IN HER OWN TIME

WINNIE MANDELA

Sharon Goulds

Hamish Hamilton
London

Many people helped with the research for this book, those in South Africa will probably never see it. I was often asked not to name names, so to all those anonymous people – thank you.

Sharon Goulds

IN HER OWN TIME

This series focuses a spotlight on women whose lives and work have all too often been overlooked yet who have made significant contributions to society in many different areas: from politics and painting to science and social reform.

Women's voices have in the past been the silent ones of history. In Britain, for example, the restrictions of society, the time-consuming nature of domestic work, and the poor educational opportunities available to women until this century, have meant that not only did women rarely have the opportunity to explore their abilities beyond those which society expected of them, but also that their aspirations and achievements were often not recorded.

This series profiles a number of women who, through a combination of character and circumstance, were able to influence ideas and attitudes or contribute to the arts and sciences. None of them were alone in their ambitions. There must have been many other women whose experiences we know nothing of because they were not recorded. Many of the 'ordinary' women who have supported the so-called 'exceptional' women of history also displayed great courage, skill and determination. Political and social change, in particular, has been accelerated by the pioneering work of individual women but rarely achieved without the collective efforts of masses of unknown women.

The work of many women in the series took them into the public eye: some were honoured and celebrated, more frequently they faced disapproval or lack of sympathy with their ideas. Many were ahead of their time and only later did their pioneering activities gain public respect. Others found their lives so deeply entangled with current events that their path was virtually chosen for them. A few were not closely involved with contemporary society but highly original characters who nevertheless influenced or informed others. By exploring the struggles, hopes, failures and achievements of these women, we can discover much about the society they lived in and how each made their personal contribution — in their own way, in their own time.

Olivia Bennett

HAMISH HAMILTON CHILDREN'S BOOKS
Published by the Penguin Group
27 Wrights Lane, London W8 5TZ, England
Viking Penguin Inc., 40 West 23rd Street, New York, New York 10010, U.S.A.
Penguin Books Australia Ltd, Ringwood, Victoria, Australia
Penguin Books Canada Ltd, 2801 John Street, Markham, Ontario, Canada L3R 1B4
Penguin Books (N.Z.) Ltd, 182–190 Wairau Road, Auckland 10, New Zealand

Penguin Books Ltd, Registered Offices: Harmondsworth, Middlesex, England

First published in Great Britain 1988 by
Hamish Hamilton Children's Books
Copyright © 1988 by Sharon Goulds

Design by Sally Boothroyd
Cover design by Clare Truscott
Map by Tony Garrett

British Library Cataloguing in Publication Data

Goulds, Sharon
Winnie Mandela.—(In her own time).
1. Mandela, Winnie—Juvenile literature
2. Black nationalism—South Africa—
Biography—Juvenile literature
I. Title   II. Series
322.4′4′0924   DT779.95.M3
ISBN 0-241-12173-6

Typeset in Palatino by Katerprint Typesetting Services, Oxford
Printed in Great Britain by
Butler & Tanner Ltd, Frome, Somerset

Contents

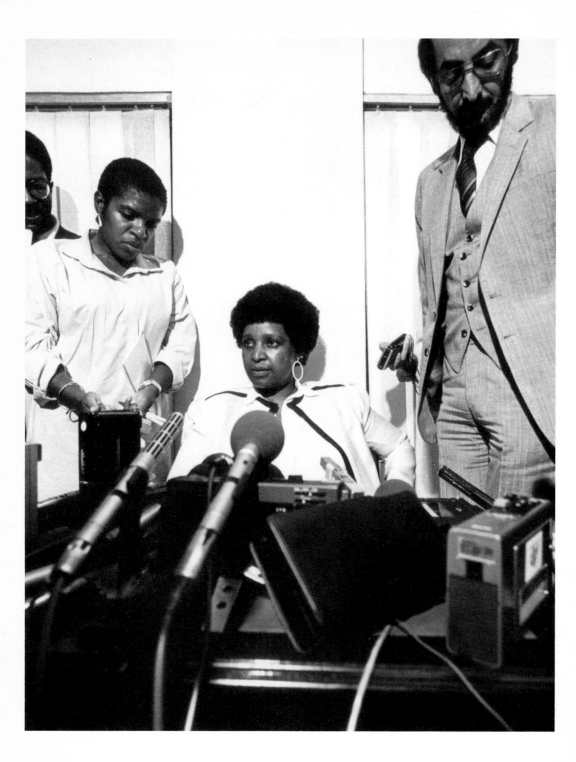

Chapter One

A Transkei Childhood

Twelve-year-old Nomzamo Winifred Madikizela was very happy. She had recently won a place at secondary school and for the first time in her life she was the proud owner of a pair of shoes. She and her father Columbus had made the long journey from their homestead into the village of Bizana to buy the new school uniform. As well as the uniform and shoes, Columbus bought Winnie a new overcoat. It was several sizes too big but Winnie was delighted with it. New clothes were a rare treat in the Madikizela family.

Winnie and her father had finished what was for Winnie the interesting part of the shopping. Her new clothes were packed away in neat parcels. Now they were in the queue at the village food store. The shop was full of local people from the surrounding hills wearing the traditional brightly coloured blankets. They stood in line, vivid splashes of colour inside the rather dingy shop. Some of the people had walked long distances to reach the shops of Bizana. Many travelled with babies and young children. As they waited, Winnie noticed a man with his wife and baby enter the store. There was no café in the area so the man bought a loaf and a soft drink for his wife while she sat and fed the baby. The young mother looked exhausted. As Winnie watched, a young white man strode out from behind the counter across to the woman and her child. He kicked at them and their food and

Winnie Mandela is used to a lot of attention from the media. South Africa is rarely out of the news and Winnie's actions and opinions are often quoted in the international press. Within South Africa, however, press censorship has all too often suppressed the voices of the black community in the fight against apartheid.

screamed at them to get out. Winnie was horrified. It was the first time she had seen anyone treated like that. Yet no one in the crowded shop raised a murmur. This was South Africa in the 1940s. The customers were black but the shop, like all the others in the village, was owned by whites.

Early life

Winnie Mandela was born Nomzamo Winifred Madikizela on 26 September 1934, in a small village in the Transkei in South Africa. Her African name Nomzamo means 'trial'; suggesting she was someone who would have a lot to put up with in life. It proved to be an apt name.

Both her parents were teachers. Her father, Columbus, could have been one of the chiefs of his tribe but chose instead to become the headmaster of a primary school. Most of the men in the rural areas wore colourful blankets but Columbus, as a headmaster, had to wear a suit. There were nine children in the Madikizela family. When Winnie was eight years old, one of her sisters, Sisi Vuyelwa, died of the lung disease tuberculosis and her mother died shortly afterwards. Her mother's funeral is one of Winnie's most vivid childhood memories. So many people turned up for it that the service was held in the open air. Two oxen and several sheep were slaughtered to feed the guests. The huts in which they lived were painted black and the windows smeared white as a sign of mourning.

After the funeral the household slowly returned to normal. Winnie's father refused the help of many willing aunts and decided to bring up the children himself. They each had their own jobs. Winnie had to leave

The village huts were neat and simple with grass roofs and mud walls. While Winnie was growing up the Transkei was known as a 'native reserve' which meant the area was for blacks only. However, some whites did live there and had taken over much of the best farmland. Jobs were scarce and black men often had to earn a living away from home in the industrial areas.

There are moments of solitude when I miss my childhood very much and the older I grow, the more I realise what effect it had on me; the love of my country. Running through those bare fields barefooted, looking after cattle, sheep and goats – that has never completely left me. Somewhere in my subconscious mind that is the country I am really fighting for.

Winnie Mandela

school for half a year to work in the fields. She milked cows, tended sheep and goats and helped with the harvest.

Despite many hardships, Winnie had a happy childhood. The land they lived in was beautiful, set among green hills and blue skies. The children were free to explore the countryside. Winnie spent hours making clay toys and model animals, which she baked in a kiln built by the older boys.

There was never a shortage of people to play with; apart from her own brothers and sisters, Winnie lived within a larger family of aunts, uncles and cousins. Three generations lived in a group of grass-roofed huts and altogether there were over twenty children. One of the family traditions was storytelling. Night after night, as they all sat round the fire in the open air eating their evening meal, the older folk would tell stories. They talked of heroes and demons, of the people who had lived in the land in earlier days, and of the arrival of the men with blue eyes, white skin and long straight hair.

Trips away from their home in eMbongweni were rare because there was no public transport. Sometimes the children would walk to their grandmother's house in the nearest village, Bizana. The journey took them a day and a half. In 1945, when the news of the end of the Second World War reached their village, Winnie and some of the other children begged a lift in a lorry to join in the victory celebrations at Bizana. They had been told that there was a party in the town hall and people were dancing and singing in the streets. They were looking forward to joining in the fun. When they arrived they found the town hall doors were closed to them because they were black. Only white people were celebrating inside. Winnie has never forgotten her sense of disappointment. The black children had to make do with scrambling on the ground outside for the oranges and sweets thrown to them. Yet when the war started thousands of black and Indian men had volunteered to fight for what they thought was a just cause. Many of them were killed, even though the South African government refused to let black or coloured men carry arms. They could only become labourers and watchmen in the white army.

Being black

Winnie was soon very conscious that the whites looked down on the blacks. Everywhere she looked whites were better off. They had better food, better clothes, better land and better houses. Winnie knew from an early age that 'there were the "have" and the "have nots" in our society' – and that it was no accident that the have nots were all black. Winnie was thirteen when, in 1948, a new Afrikaner government came into power. It introduced the term apartheid, and organised more tightly the system designed to keep blacks and whites apart. They intended to make sure that the whites continued to get the better deal.

School history books always portray the white invasion of South Africa as the triumph of civilised godfearing men over a horde of barbaric savages. But through her father Winnie learnt that there was another sort of history, which took a different view of what had happened. Columbus would say, 'Now, the book says this, but the truth is these white people invaded our country and stole the land from our grandfathers.'

I became aware at an early age that the whites felt superior to us. And I could see how shabby my father looked in comparison with white teachers. That hurts your pride when you are a child.

Winnie Mandela,
Part of My Soul

11

Chapter Two

Early History

Winnie learnt that two thousand years ago, the Khoi-khoi and the San people lived in Southern Africa. We know they herded sheep and cattle and made pottery. During the Iron Age, trade with the outside world began and by the eleventh century gold, ivory and other minerals from Southern Africa were in great demand in Arabia, India and China.

The Thembu (the clan to which Nelson Mandela belongs) seem to have appeared in the area in the sixteenth century. The Xhosa clan, whose descendants also live in South Africa today, started to move south in 1600. Fifty-two years later the Netherlands East

Robben Island in Table Bay has been used as a prison for over three hundred years. The first people to be detained there were two African leaders called Herry and Doman, imprisoned by the Dutch in 1660.

India Company established a trading station at Table Bay. This new station supplied the company's ships, on their way to Asia, with water, vegetables and meat. In 1659–60 the first of many wars broke out between the Dutch and the Africans as the Dutch began to move out of the trading station and settle on Khoi-khoi land, starting to grow crops and herd cattle.

By 1800 there were 22,000 Dutch, or Boers as they came to be called, living in a colony which extended as far as 1000 kilometers from Cape Town. The Boers had also brought in about 25,000 slaves from the East. As the settlers expanded there were more clashes with the Africans (Khoisan) whose land was being stolen. Despite efforts to resist the invaders, who were much better armed, by 1799 there were no independent Khoisan left in Cape Colony. They had all become servants on Dutch settler farms.

The British captured the Cape from the Dutch in 1795. Cape Colony officially became a British possession in the general European peace settlement of 1815. The British and the Boers were always quarrelling. In an attempt to get away from British rule, the Boers started to trek into the interior. They were resisted fiercely by the Zulus, still the most powerful military force in the area. The Zulus fought bravely but the Boers had guns and horses; the Zulus had only spears. They were defeated at the Battle of Blood River in Natal in 1838. The Boers continued the Great Trek into the Orange Free State and the Transvaal. Here the British left them largely alone. The Boers continued to take land from the local people, although they were successfully opposed by the Sotho people in 1858 under their king Moshoeshoe.

King Moshoeshoe of the Sotho (c.1785–1870) was successful in battle against both the British and Boers. His people were prosperous farmers exporting maize, wheat and cattle to the Cape Colony and elsewhere. It was only advancing old age which forced him to appeal, in 1868, for British protection.

THE SCRAMBLE FOR AFRICA

Between 1867 and 1885 diamonds and the largest concentration of gold in the world were found in the Orange Free State and the Transvaal. This discovery increased European activity in the area and made the land even more valuable to them. In 1871 Britain annexed the diamond area of Kimberley, ignoring protests from the Boers and the Griqua people whose land it was. From the start the mining industry was built on cheap African labour. The rapid growth of the gold and diamond industries meant more conflict between the white settlers of Dutch origin and those of English origin. In 1899 the situation got so bad that war broke out.

The war between the two white peoples of South Africa lasted over two years. Its effect on the blacks, who were being forced to become increasingly dependent on white bosses and white-owned mines, was considerable. According to the African diarist Sol Plaatje, black miners from the Rand area were 'reduced to digging up dead dogs for food'. Britain, with the might of the Empire behind her, was eventually victorious.

THE UNION OF SOUTH AFRICA

In 1910 Britain granted independence to the new Union of South Africa. The constitution gave rights to the white English and Afrikaner (as the Boers now called themselves) population and excluded Africans and other non-whites. The blacks protested but were ignored. Except for some in Cape Province, blacks did not have the vote. The Native Lands Act in 1913 barred blacks from owning land in three quarters of the national territory. In industry, blacks were banned from skilled and supervisory

When the [Afrikaner] Nationalist government first came to power in 1948, they were welcomed in a strange way by black people: 'We prefer the Boer' they said. This was not said with any affection . . . The Boer [Afrikaner] was preferred to the hypocritical English of whom it was said they smiled at you with their front teeth and chewed you with their back teeth. The Boer would hate nakedly, would express his evil and prejudice nakedly and would be a blunt, brutal final death on the land.

Bessie Head

jobs. A white worker earned over ten times more than a black. A white could go on strike, a black could not.

In 1912 the blacks set up the South African Native National Congress to try to make sure their voice was heard. In 1923 this organisation was renamed the African National Congress (ANC). They adopted a national flag; green for the land, black for the people, gold for the riches and a National anthem 'Nkosi Sikelel'iAfrika' (Lord Bless Africa).

Throughout the twenties and thirties successive white governments passed more and more anti-black laws. At the end of the Second World War, white South Africans put the Afrikaner National Party in power. They had campaigned under the slogan 'apartheid', promising to ensure white domination.

Nkosi Sikel'i Afrika
God Bless Africa
Malupakam'upondo lwayo
Raise up her spirit
Yiva imitandazo yetu
Hear our prayers
Usi-Sikelele
And Bless Us.

National Anthem

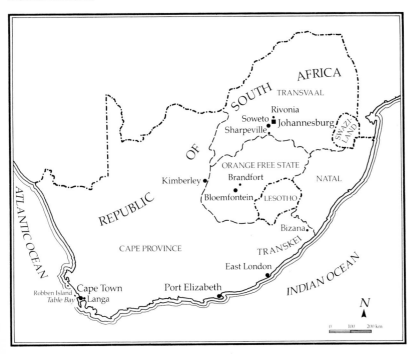

15

Dr Hendrik Verwoerd was known as the Grand Architect of Apartheid. He was responsible for the Bantu Education Act and was determined that 'the Natives will be taught from childhood that equality with Europeans is not for them . . . People who believe in equality are not desirable teachers for natives.'

1948 APARTHEID

The word apartheid literally means 'apartness'. The new regime brought in a whole set of laws that would push black and white further and further apart. It also invented the category 'coloured' to classify anyone whom it said was neither black nor white.

In 1949 the ban on marriages between black and white was extended to include marriages between whites and coloureds. A year later the government began to register people according to their so-called race and to insist that black, white and coloured live in different parts of the cities and countryside. Black women were forced, like black men, to carry pass books to prove that they had permission even to be in a white area. In 1953 the National Government 'reformed' black education, until then mostly carried out by missionaries. Black schools were to teach a different, and decidedly inferior, syllabus from white schools.

Black opposition had begun to build up. A new generation of political activists revitalised the ANC. In 1944 the Youth League was founded; founder members included Nelson Mandela, Walter Sisulu and Oliver Tambo, all future leaders of the ANC.

The struggle for equal rights has continued throughout the last forty years. Winnie Mandela's life, and the lives of many thousands of others, is totally intertwined with the history of this struggle and that of the country she lives in. Hers is the story we explore but the irrepressible courage it reveals is typical of many black South Africans whose stories remain untold.

Chapter Three

Winnie at School

Winnie was always a good student. She, and all the others in her village, had to walk miles, barefoot, to get to school. There were buses for white children but not blacks. Education for whites, unlike black education, was compulsory — and free. White schools were housed in modern buildings with up-to-date equipment. Black schools received very little government money and black parents had to pay. Winnie's father was supposed to expel children whose parents could not afford the fees but whenever he could he paid for them himself. In the Madikizela household the importance of a good education was always emphasised.

Although Winnie had lost more than half a year's schooling during her final year at primary school, she passed the examination

Black schools in South Africa were underfunded when Winnie was a child and they still are. For every pound spent on a black pupil, seven is spent on a white one.

Sometimes when it rains
I think of times
When I watched goats
Running so fast from the rain
While sheep seemed to enjoy
* it*

Sometimes when it rains
I think of times
When we had to undress
Carry the small bundle of
* uniforms and books*
On our heads
And cross the river after
* school*

Gcina Mhlope,
Sometimes When It Rains

which took her up to secondary school. The following year she went on to Shawbury High School, a church school run by the Methodists in Qumbu some way from Winnie's home. It was a particularly good school and Columbus, who was impressed by Winnie's academic achievements, was determined that she should go there even though it meant being a boarder.

Winnie's school fees placed a great financial strain on Columbus. Winnie's elder sister Nancy also contributed, leaving school herself to take on odd jobs. Winnie studied hard, conscious of the debt she owed her father and sister. She is described by one of her old school friends as 'very reserved'. Yet her qualities of leadership were apparent even then. In her last year she was elected head prefect. When she went home for the holidays, Winnie often took friends with her. She realises now that she was putting more strain on the family budget, for she was in the habit of promising less well-off friends that her father could pay her fees.

The outside world

At Shawbury High School Winnie came into contact with the political issues of the day. Many of her teachers were graduates of Fort Hare University College, which had produced several black political leaders. Her final years at school, in the early fifties, were a very eventful time in South African politics. In 1952 Nelson Mandela and other African National Congress leaders had organised a campaign against apartheid known as the Defiance Campaign. All over the country volunteers burnt their passes in public, entered areas reserved for other races and took no notice of the 'Europeans Only' signs

People who burned their passes as part of the Defiance Campaign risked imprisonment. Black people have to carry passes at all times. Failure to produce your pass when asked to means that you can be sent to jail.

in stations and shops. White supporters went into black ghetto areas without the written permission they were supposed to have. The campaign attracted tremendous support and ANC membership increased from 7000 to 100,000. Initially the campaign was non-violent but in November police fired on African crowds in Port Elizabeth, East London and Kimberley. Only then was there a violent reaction.

At Winnie's school the ANC leaders were looked up to as heroes. The pupils were desperate to show their support and many came out on strike. Shawbury School hit the headlines. In those days a school strike, now a commonplace event in South Africa, was unheard of. People were horrified that school children should behave like this. Many of the pupils were sent home. Only those who were writing their final exams were allowed to stay at the school. Despite all these distractions Winnie got a first class pass.

The City of Gold

For some time now, inspired by her father, Winnie had set her heart on becoming a social worker. He was convinced that this was the ideal career for her. Columbus had found out about the Hofmeyr School in Johannesburg, which was the only place in South Africa where blacks could train as social workers. Winnie applied and was offered a place. It was quite an achievement. She was the first scholar from the countryside to be taken on.

The bustling city of Johannesburg was likely to be a huge shock to anyone used to the quiet beauty of rural Transkei. Winnie had never been out of the area and had never been on a train. Throughout her holiday she was besieged by advice from well meaning relatives, all very concerned about her fate in 'Egoli', the City of Gold, as Johannesburg was called.

She was escorted to the city by two young male relatives who were going to work as migrant labourers in the gold mines. In the Transkei there was so much poverty and so few jobs that most men were forced to find work elsewhere, either in the mines or the sugar plantations. They would be away from home for a year, living twenty to a room in men-only hostels in special compounds.

At Johannesburg Winnie said goodbye to her cousins and waited on the noisy station platform, 'so shocked I literally just stood there for an hour'. She eventually started to make her way through the station. People stared at her:

'I was carrying my provisions in a cardboard box . . . I put it on my head and carried my trunk on my side . . . I was a country girl, to me there was nothing wrong with carrying a cardboard box on my head.'

She knew that someone from the college would be there to meet her and was relieved when two white women came up to her. They drove Winnie through the streets of Johannesburg. She had never seen anything like it. People everywhere, hustling and bustling, and the noise of voices and traffic filling the air. It was early morning but the wide streets were already crowded. The cars, the shops, the buildings, were unlike anything in the Transkei. Winnie was petrified. 'I had never seen so many people in my life at one time.'

Columbus had booked Winnie into the Helping Hand Hostel in the heart of Johannesburg. It had been set up specially to cater for black women on their own in the city. Columbus knew they would look after his daughter. Winnie was to live there for four and a half years.

Soweto (SOuth WEstern TOwnship) covers about eighty-five square kilometres. The basic Soweto home has four small rooms usually without a bath or shower. Recently the residents have refused to pay the rent in an attempt to force the authorities to modernise and repair the houses, which are all rented from the council.

Black and white

In Johannesburg Winnie was brought face to face with the contrast between the wealth and opportunities available to white South Africans and the conditions of the blacks. Most people in her hostel belonged to the ANC and to various trade union movements. Winnie found that all the women were very well informed about political affairs. They were constantly discussing political issues. She was determined not to be left out and started doing some serious political reading.

Despite all these new excitements Winnie had to concentrate on her studies. Her father was paying for her course. Winnie knew how hard this was for him and she was determined to win a scholarship. The college was also anxious about her progress. As the first rural student they had taken on, Winnie was an experiment for them. The fate of other applicants from the rural areas depended to some extent on how well she did. Winnie was under a lot of pressure. Nevertheless she won her scholarship and emerged as one of the Hofmeyr School's star pupils.

During her social work course Winnie had her first glimpse of Soweto. Little did she know that this sprawling smokey ghetto was to be her future home. At this time Soweto, which is twenty-seven kilometres outside Johannesburg, had no electricity. Everybody had to use paraffin and coal fires for cooking and heating, which meant that a permanent fog hung over the township. About a million people lived in cramped surroundings in houses which were more like Portakabins. Black people working in Johannesburg were not allowed to live anywhere else. Even Winnie's hostel was shortly to close down.

Life in Soweto starts at about 4 a.m. Mind you, Soweto is never sleepy. There is the in and out movement of the workers who do shift work. The sonorous row of fast moving trains running in and out every minute to collect workers is heard from 4 a.m. and dies out just after midnight.

Imagine, at the crack of dawn, the haze of greyish-brown smoke enshrouding the ghetto. It indicates that inside the matchbox houses the inmates have woken up. The one whose turn it is – be it father, mother, daughter or son – jumps out of the blankets first to light the coal-stove, and thus the smoke belches from each chimney engulfing the ghetto.

Joyce Sikakane,
A Window on Soweto

Chapter Four

Winnie and Nelson

Winnie graduated in the autumn of 1955, winning the prize for the best student. She was delighted when the Baragwanath Hospital in Soweto offered her a job as their first black medical social worker. But then she was offered a scholarship to study sociology in America with all expenses paid. Choosing which to take up was a difficult decision. After much deliberation, Winnie accepted the hospital job.

As a social worker Winnie was particularly aware of the conditions under which her people lived: 'I dealt with hunger, with poverty directly, I was involved with my community'. She had done field work in the Transkei and had come across great poverty there, but was even more shocked by the hardship she found in Johannesburg's townships. The poverty some people suffered was in sharp contrast to the wealth and high standard of living that the City of Gold could and did provide for others.

Part of Winnie's job was to visit new mothers and their babies after they had left hospital. She found that parents had neither the money nor the knowledge to provide the best for their children. Many had no proper homes to go to but lived in shacks made of corrugated iron and cardboard. Many of the children did not get enough to eat. Often young mothers struggled to support their families alone. In several cases the fathers were migrant workers forced to leave their families in the rural areas and find work in

I had started my work in urban communities where families, by and large, were a complete unit, with a mother, a father and children. This gave me a false picture of what to expect in the rural areas, where I soon found that more than three-quarters of the families were without husbands and fathers. They were away from home, gone on migrant labour contracts to one industrial area or another. This was a shocking revelation to me.

Ellen Kuzwayo,
Hungry in a Rich Land

Johannesburg. Lonely, separated from their wives and children, they formed relationships with the women they met in Soweto. Of course their meagre salaries could never support the two families. One or other of the mothers would almost always be left to support their children as best they could. The laws of apartheid – that make it impossible for a contract worker to bring his family to the city – cause a lot of heartache and trap many families in extreme poverty.

The Freedom Charter

We the people of South Africa declare for all our country and the world to know: that South Africa belongs to all who live in it, black and white, and that no government can justly claim authority unless it is based on the will of the people.

The Freedom Charter

While Winnie became increasingly aware, and angry, at the way apartheid affected people's lives, and tried her best to help them as a social worker, others were taking political steps. 1955 had been a particularly active year for the African National Congress. In June they had called a Congress of the People. More than 3000 South Africans, black, brown and white, adopted the Freedom Charter. It summed up the hopes of black South Africa. Its statement of basic human rights was what they were all working to achieve.

Meanwhile the Afrikaner Government had not been idle. They drew up laws that increasingly restricted the movements and freedoms of black people. Many of the ANC leaders were under continual 'banning' orders. These prevented them from speaking at meetings or seeing each other. They could not be quoted in newspapers or magazines. By imposing these orders, the government tried to silence unwanted opposition and dissent. The government also announced that from 1956 African women would have to carry passes, stating who they were, where they came from and where they were supposed to live. Men had been carrying these passes for years.

Eventually over three hundred apartheid laws were passed. The Bantu Education Act legislated separate education for blacks, the Group Areas Act drew up racial zones. These controlled where blacks, coloureds and whites could live. There were separate beaches for black and white, separate buses and trains, separate parks, sports grounds, cinemas and taxis.

The Congress of the People was, in Nelson Mandela's words, 'a spectacular and moving occasion'. Despite the presence of Special Branch detectives, who took photographs and searched both audience and speakers for documents, the crowd remained good humoured.

The courtship begins

Winnie was still living in the hostel at Jeppe Street, in the section reserved for working women. She shared a ten-bed dormitory with women from widely different backgrounds. Winnie soon made friends with Adelaide Tsukudu. Adelaide was a staff nurse at Baragwanath and she was going out with Oliver Tambo, a leader of the ANC. Oliver was also a lawyer in partnership with Nelson Mandela. Winnie's first glimpse of Nelson had been in court. He was defending a friend of hers who had been beaten up by the police. Winnie remembers her first impression – it was of a 'towering, imposing man, quite awe-inspiring'.

Early in 1956 Oliver introduced Winnie to Nelson. Soon afterwards she received a telephone call and an invitation to lunch. She was terrified – and quite certain she had nothing to wear. He was several years older than her and suddenly all her clothes seemed very schoolgirlish. She borrowed something from a friend, hoping it made her look older and more dignified. Nelson took Winnie for an Indian meal. Poor Winnie – it was her first taste of curry: 'It was such a struggle to eat. I couldn't swallow. I was almost in tears because of this hot, hot curry. And he noticed and embarrassingly gave me a glass of water and said, "If you find it too hot, it helps to take a sip of water".'

Throughout the meal Nelson was constantly interrupted by people coming to ask his advice. When they left the restaurant, Winnie remembers, it took about half an hour to reach Nelson's car which was parked just outside — 'Nelson couldn't walk from here to there without having consultations.'

Right from the beginning Winnie had to

Even at that stage, life with him was a life without him. He did not even pretend that I would have a special claim to his time.

Winnie Mandela,
Part of My Soul

share Nelson with his political and legal work. There was no time for romance. When they met, Nelson, along with 155 others, was out on bail facing charges of high treason. The Treason Trial was to drag on for four years before the defendants were finally acquitted. On their first date Nelson asked Winnie to help raise money to cover the legal costs.

A proposal of marriage

One day they were driving along when Nelson pulled up on the side of the road and said 'You know, there is a woman, a dressmaker, you must go and see her, she is going to make your wedding gown. How many bridesmaids would you like to have?' That was Winnie's proposal of marriage. All she managed to say in reply was 'What time?'

Nelson had been married before. He was aware of the strain that his lifestyle and political commitment could put on any relationship. He did point out to Winnie the disadvantages of living with a man who was constantly hounded by the police. She soon realised that his fight against apartheid came before anything else in his life. But 'I was madly in love with him at that stage and so was he with me in his own way'.

Nelson was banned from leaving Johannesburg so he could not ask formal permission of Winnie's father. Winnie had to go herself. The family were proud that such an important man as Nelson Mandela wished to marry Winnie but they were worried too. Her father was concerned that Winnie would not be able to cope with Nelson's three children by his first marriage. He also warned her 'you are marrying the struggle, not the man'. History proved him right.

TREASON TRIAL

The ACCUSED

DECEMBE 1956

The 155 people accused with Nelson Mandela of high treason came from all walks of life: drivers, clerks, factory workers, labourers, teachers and housewives. There were 105 blacks, twenty-three whites, twenty-one Indians and seven coloured people. In jail they were segregated according to their colour.

27

Chapter 5

The Struggle, Not The Man

On 14 June 1958, Nelson and Winnie were married in the Transkei. Nelson had been granted four days permission to leave Johannesburg. 'I insisted on getting married at home because nothing could have pleased my father better and I wanted Nelson to see my background,' explained Winnie. The Mandelas have still not completed their wedding in the traditional way. After the service in the bride's home the couple are supposed to go to the groom's home to be married there also. But Nelson's pass was too short and they had to rush back to

. . . there was never any kind of life that I can recall as a family life, as a young bride's life, where you sit down with your husband and dream dreams . . . You just couldn't tear Nelson from the people, from the struggle. The nation came first.

Winnie Mandela,
Part of My Soul.

Nelson and Winnie on their wedding day.

Johannesburg. Winnie is determined to complete the ceremony one day. She still has part of the wedding cake awaiting Nelson's release from prison.

Back in Johannesburg Winnie and Nelson went to live in Nelson's house in Soweto. It was hardly the start of 'normal' married life. Each morning Nelson had to attend court in Pretoria for the Treason Trial. Often he stayed there overnight, discussing the charges with the lawyers. When he did come home it was usually for a quick bath and out again for a meeting with the ANC leaders. Winnie literally had to force him to eat. As soon as he sat down the phone would ring, somebody would ask for his help as a lawyer and off he would go, his plate untouched.

Winnie herself was becoming increasingly politically involved, separately from Nelson, both in the ANC Women's League and in the Federation of South African Women. She always says that it was the women she met in these organisations rather than her husband who helped shape her political ideas. Two women were particularly close to Winnie. Lilian Ngoyi was President both of the Women's League and of the Federation of South African Women and she organised the resistance campaigns of the women from 1952 onwards. Helen Joseph was a white social worker whom Winnie describes as 'more than a mother to me'. The friendship between Helen and Winnie continues to this day. Winnie also remembers her husband's secretary, Ruth Mompati, with much gratitude; 'I was a young girl from the countryside and she was much more modern than I was and much more sophisticated and she taught me about urban society and urban women's politics.'

Lilian Ngoyi was one of the accused in the Treason Trial and spent ten years from October 1962–November 1972 restricted to her house in Soweto. Lilian died in 1980, just before the end of another five-year banning order.

It was a struggle really because my husband was always in jail. I have always been a bread winner . . . my first arrest was in 1958, it was when we were fighting against the extension of passes to women. We went to jail but fortunately we were discharged by the court of law. If I had been sentenced it would have meant losing my job and being struck off from the nursing register.

Albertina Sisulu, 1987
(Her husband, Walter, is in prison for life. Mrs. Sisulu still runs a clinic in Soweto)

In prison

Soon after her marriage, and pregnant with their first child, Winnie took part in a mass protest against the pass laws, which were to include women for the first time. Failure to produce the pass could result in a prison sentence. The women gathered peaceably in Johannesburg to make their protest, many with their children. Over a thousand were arrested, including Winnie. It was her first experience of imprisonment but her time as a social worker had prepared her for it: 'I had spent almost three years doing my practical work as a young social worker trying to help people who were in and out of prison . . . so it was an experience I had learned to know as part of a black person's life'. While in prison Winnie nearly had a miscarriage. Luckily one of her fellow prisoners, Albertina Sisulu, whose husband was another prominent ANC leader, was a trained midwife and her skill saved the baby.

In October 1956, 20,000 women demonstrated against the extension of the pass laws to include them. They delivered their petition to the Union Building in Pretoria and then stood for half an hour in silence. Then, at a sign from Lilian Ngoyi, they began to sing, 'Now you have touched a woman you have struck a rock. You have dislodged a boulder, you will be crushed'.

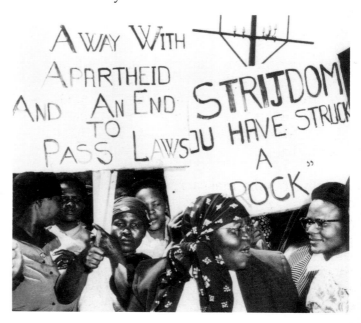

Winnie spent a fortnight in prison. When she came out she found her political activities had cost her her job. Her salary had been very important, as Nelson's frequent court appearances meant that he earned very little. Winnie's dismissal did not go unnoticed. There were several newspaper reports about the sacking of a star pupil from the Jan Hofmeyr School of Social Work. This publicity resulted in Winnie being offered another job by the Johannesburg Child Welfare Society. Winnie continued to work there after the birth of her daughter Zeni.

Sharpeville

In 1960 something happened which changed the nature of black protest for ever. It was the year of Sharpeville. In this black township about eighty kilometres south of Johannesburg police fired at a peaceable crowd of men, women and children who were protesting against the pass laws. Sixty-nine were killed and 176 injured. A friend came to give Winnie the news:

> 'The people were laughing and chatting. It was like a holiday,' she said, 'then suddenly I heard these shots, shots, shots, shots. Everyone was screaming and pushing madly to get away but the police kept firing'.

The Sharpeville massacre had a profound effect on the confrontation between black and white in South Africa. To many people, the police shootings made a mockery of the ANC policy of non-violence. It was not the first time in South African history that the police had opened fire. But this time the world knew about it. Abroad, people began to lose

Helen Joseph at her garden gate while under house arrest in 1962. Helen was born in England in 1905 and went to South Africa in 1931. She and Lilian Ngoyi played a major part in organising the mass demonstration of women against the pass laws in 1956.

It was a meeting, mind, not even a demonstration, at Sharpeville. If you could have seen that, the women lying dead with their children on their backs, it was terrible. Shot with their children on their backs. Lying dead.

Albertina Sisulu

The massacre at Sharpeville brought the issue of apartheid to the world's attention and it led to a greater militancy among black people. The two major political organisations, the ANC and the Pan Africanist Congress, both formed military sections, as a direct response to the violence of the police.

confidence in the South African Government. They were appalled by the brutal action of the police and worried that South Africa might no longer be a safe place in which to do business. In South Africa itself people from all over the country expressed their horror at what had happened. Demonstrations followed and fourteen more people were killed by police in the black township of Langa near Cape Town.

State of Emergency

The government's response was to declare a State of Emergency. Political organisations like the ANC and the Pan Africanist Congress were banned. Two thousand activists were detained, including Nelson Mandela who was kept in Pretoria prison. Oliver Tambo had already been sent to Britain and Tanzania to set up ANC offices abroad.

Meanwhile the Treason Trial continued. By now there were only thirty defendants left from the original 156. Over the three years of the trial, charges against the others had been dropped. Now the defence lawyers resigned. They said it was impossible to conduct a political trial during a State of Emergency. Nelson and another lawyer also standing trial took over and prepared their colleagues for the continuing case. In court Nelson made an important statement:

> 'We are not anti-white, we are against white supremacy and, in struggling against white supremacy we have the support of some sections of the European population . . . It is quite clear that the ANC has consistently preached a policy of race harmony and we have condemned racialism no matter by whom it is professed'.

After five months in prison Nelson came home to Winnie and Zeni. Their second daughter Zindzi was born in December. The months between September 1960 and March 1961 were all the Mandelas were to know of family life. At the end of March the Treason Trial came to an end. Everyone was found not guilty. For the first time in ten years Nelson was not under a banning order and was able to attend public meetings and speak freely. However, Nelson knew that he would not be allowed to enjoy his new freedom for long. He had decided to go 'underground'. He did come home from the courtroom but Winnie did not even have a chance to congratulate him on the verdict. 'He was outside the gate, but I couldn't reach him, there were so many people wishing him well – everybody was excited. I packed his bag, but by the time I took it out he wasn't there. He was gone. Someone else came to fetch the bag about an hour later . . . That was the last time I saw my husband as a family man, legally at home. There had been no chance to sit down and discuss his decision to commit himself totally.'

Chapter 6

Being Alone

Nelson had realised that the authorities
would never allow him to operate freely. The
only hope was to work in secret. In an open
letter to the press he explained that going
'underground' was the only course left open
to him: 'I have had to separate myself from
my own dear wife and children, from my
mother and sisters, to live as an outlaw in my
own land. I have had to abandon my
profession and live in poverty as many of my
people are doing . . . The struggle is my life.'

For Winnie these were extremely difficult
days. Nelson had tried in practical ways to
ease his departure for her. She found that he
had paid six months rent in advance and the
car had been repaired. But nothing could
prepare her for the loneliness. Despite the
help of many friends she felt very vulnerable
without her husband's support. She explains
that in her culture men and women are
prepared for different roles: '. . . there is
usually a huge gap between our husbands
and ourselves . . . the tendency was to rather
educate the boys in our society and the
woman belonged to the kitchen . . . you were
never prepared for a double role where you
would be head of a family and a mother at
the same time.' Winnie had, in fact, to take
on a third role as a political leader in Nelson's
absence and, despite her fears, proved quite
capable of adding that to the roles of mother
and head of the family.

It was during this period of her life that
Winnie rejoined the Anglican Church.

Religion had been a strong influence in her childhood and it was to comfort her throughout the coming years.

The knock at the window
While Nelson, who became known as the Black Pimpernel, travelled the country keeping people in touch with the banned ANC, the security police watched Winnie like hawks. They knew that Nelson would attempt to see his family. 'We had a very dramatic life. I waited for that sacred knock at the window in the early hours of the morning. I never knew when. I never had an appointment made. At the beginning he used to come for an hour or so early in the morning, depending on the political situation. Later they were watching me twenty-four hours a day and I had to slip out between police cordons to go to him.'

Winnie with her two daughters, Zeni, born in 1959 and Zindzi, born in December 1960.

These meetings between Winnie and Nelson were very complicated arrangements. Sometimes Winnie would have to change cars ten times before reaching her husband. Many of these rendezvous were organised by white friends. They had some narrow escapes. Once Winnie, travelling in a doctor's car, was stopped at a road block. She was rather plump at the time and looked convincingly pregnant. Winnie just lay back and began to fake labour pains, 'I was gasping and sweating and they let us through'.

Nelson became a master of disguises. Sometimes Winnie herself did not recognise him straightaway. On one occasion Winnie was waiting at some traffic lights. She just happened to glance across at the car next to her and suddenly realised that the 'chauffeur' driving it was Nelson.

The ANC rented a farm in Rivonia, on the outskirts of Johannesburg, where Winnie was able to meet Nelson with the children. Here they had some sort of family life. Nelson

Damaged pylons, a result of Umkhonto We Sizwe's sabotage campaign: 'We of Umkhonto have always sought — as the liberation movement has sought — to achieve liberation without bloodshed and civil clash . . . we hope that we will bring the government to its senses before it is too late'.

could play with his children and take them for walks in the large garden. For years Zeni, who was then about two and a half, imagined Lilliesleaf Farm was her real home.

Last days of freedom

After ten months travelling around South Africa, Nelson left the country to make a tour of the African states. He also came to London to meet British politicians. Nelson has said of this trip that for the first time in his life he felt free:

> 'Wherever I went I was treated like a human being. In the African states I saw black and white mingling peacefully and happily in hotels, cinemas; trading in the same areas, using the same public transport and living in the same residential areas.'

On his return to South Africa, Nelson was even more of a marked man. Just before his departure the ANC had abandoned their tradition of non-violent struggle. They had set up Umkhonto we Sizwe, which means 'Spear of the Nation', as a guerilla group. Under Nelson's leadership, Umkhonto was to carry out a campaign of sabotage against carefully chosen targets. It was a difficult decision but 'Might' seemed the only argument that whites would listen to. The policy was to attack buildings and military installations, not people. On the 16 December 1961 Umkhonto we Sizwe members exploded bombs at targets in Johannesburg, Durban and Port Elizabeth. The only person killed was one of the people planting the bombs.

Meetings between Nelson and Winnie became even more difficult to organise. Stand-ins for Winnie were frequently used to

Now having spent more than half his adult life, more than a quarter of a century, behind bars, he [Nelson Mandela] has become the living symbol of his movement and the personification of the bondage of his people, most of whom could never have seen or heard him.

Joseph Lelyveld,
Move Your Shadow

confuse the authorities. Winnie travelled by ambulance to their final meeting. She pretended to be a woman in labour accompanied by a white-coated doctor. Her two anxious little girls were with her. The police at each road block were completely taken in by Winnie's performance. Shortly after that meeting Nelson was captured, on 5 August 1962, apparently due to a tip-off from an informer. It was to be twenty-two years before Winnie could even touch her husband again, for when she visited him in prison, they were always separated from each other by a thick glass barrier and had to talk through a telephone system.

Nelson was charged with encouraging Africans to strike and with leaving the country without valid travel documents. He was found guilty and sentenced to five years with hard labour. Winnie was present in court. She was shocked – not just for herself and her family, but also for the political struggle, 'and what it meant for the cause of my people'. She did not let her shock show but left the court room vowing to 'continue the fight as I have always done in the past'.

Banned

Shortly after Nelson's imprisonment Winnie received her first banning order. She had become increasingly politically active, now she was forbidden to attend public meetings or social gatherings. She could not write for publication or be quoted in a magazine or newspaper. She was forbidden to go into any 'educational establishment', which meant that she was never allowed inside her own children's school. Winnie was to spend the best part of the next twenty-five years under various banning orders.

Chapter Seven

Part of My Soul

Winnie found it hard enough to come to terms with her husband's imprisonment but there was worse to come. The police raided the ANC hide-out at Lilliesleaf Farm in Rivonia. They arrested Walter Sisulu and several other leading members of the ANC. They also discovered a pile of incriminating documents. The opening of the Rivonia Trial in December 1963 found Nelson in court again as Accused No. 1. He and seven others were charged with nearly twenty acts of sabotage and with conspiracy to overthrow the government by revolution. The death sentence hung over them.

The pressure on Winnie at this time was intense. She got up at dawn to feed and dress the children. She would drop them off on the way to the office, arriving there as early as she could in order to do some work before driving to Pretoria to listen to the case and have a few words with her husband. She would then rush the fifty-six kilometres back to Johannesburg in order to pick up her children and be home by 6 p.m. Winnie's banning order meant that she had to be in her own home between 6 p.m. and 6 a.m. The trial went on for months. The defendants knew that they would probably be found guilty but thought that they could at least make people aware of the struggle they were engaged in. When Nelson addressed the court he did not deny the charges of sabotage but tried to explain why they had resorted to violence:

39

'I did not plan it in a spirit of recklessness, nor because I have any love of violence. I planned it as a result of a calm and sober assessment of the political situation that had arisen after many years of tyranny, exploitation and oppression of my people by the whites.'

Nelson spoke for four hours. He commanded total attention. Albertina Sisulu, whose husband, Walter, was also on trial, remembers the atmosphere – 'it was so quiet you could hear a pin drop.' When Nelson had finished his speech he looked up at the judge and said quietly:

'During my lifetime I have dedicated myself to the struggle of the African people. I have fought against white domination, and I have fought against black domination. I have cherished the ideal of a democratic and free society in which all persons live together in harmony and with equal opportunities. It is an ideal which I hope to live for and to achieve. But if needs be, it is an ideal for which I am prepared to die.'

The court was full of international observers. Nelson's statement echoed around the world. On 11 June the Judge found all but one of the defendants guilty. The following day he sentenced them to life imprisonment.

Winnie emerged from that courtroom unbeaten. People had expected tears, 'But, no, she appeared on the steps and flashed a smile that dazzled. The effect was regal and almost triumphant, performed in the heart of the Afrikaner capital in her moment of anguish.' (Allister Sparks, *The Observer*). The crowds cheered. Winnie and her children

▶ *Around the world there was a surge of protest against the verdict in the Rivonia Trial. It was probably the international attention that saved the defendants from the death penalty.*

40

The Cape Argus

FOUNDED 1857 ★ ★ ★   CAPE TOWN, THURSDAY, JUNE 11, 1964   REGISTERED AT THE G.P.O. AS A NEWSPAPER   PRICE 3c

EIGHT GUILTY IN RIVONIA TRIAL

MRS. WINNIE MANDELA, wife of Nelson Mandela, leads her mother-in-law out of the court after the verdict as the crowd shouts slogans and marches up and down.

Seven on all four charges and one on one count

BERNSTEIN FREED, REARRESTED

The Argus Correspondent

PRETORIA, Thursday.

SEVEN of the nine accused in the Rivonia sabotage trial were found guilty on all four counts in the Supreme Court, Pretoria, to-day.

The Judge President of the Transvaal (Mr. Justice Quartus de Wet) found that one accused, Ahmed Mohamed Kathrada, a Johannesburg Indian, was guilty on one count.

He found that Lionel Gabriel Bernstein, a Johannesburg architect, was not guilty and he was discharged. Before Bernstein could leave the court he was rearrested to the magnificent cry of his wife, Hilda.

MR. JUSTICE Q. DE WET, the Transvaal Judge President.

ACTION THREAT AGAINST DRIVER

BERNSTEIN IN RAND COURT TO-MORROW

Judge's reasons

No sentence to-day

Kantor's discharge

Clearing

MRS. BERNSTEIN AND DAUGHTER IN TEARS

Natives shout and sing outside the court

The Argus Correspondent

PRETORIA, Thursday.

LED by Mrs. Albertina Sisulu, wife of Walter Sisulu, a crowd of Natives marched up to the front of the Supreme Court here about 10 minutes before the Rivonia judgement was due to be given.

WIFE HEARD THE VERDICT

MRS. LIONEL BERNSTEIN and her daughter Toni were in court to hear the verdict.

DEATH PENALTY FOR SABOTAGE TRAINING?

The Argus Parliamentary Staff

THE DEATH PENALTY will be extended to people who have undergone sabotage training — or even 'attempted, consented or taken any steps' to undergo training — within South Africa's borders, in terms of a new General Law Amendment Bill published in the Assembly to-day.

ROADBLOCKS ON ROUTES TO PRETORIA

The Argus Correspondent

JOHANNESBURG, Thursday.

ACCUSED MEN TIRED AND NERVOUS

PRETORIA, Thursday.

Mr. Justice Quartus de Wet, Judge President of the Transvaal, stopped into the Supreme Court to give the Rivonia case judgement at exactly 10 o'clock to-day.

joined the thousands of people waiting for their last glimpse of the convicted men. As they were driven off to Pretoria Central Prison, Nelson and the other leaders were accompanied by the sound of freedom songs and of the forbidden black national anthem, 'Nkosi Sikelel'iAfrika' (Lord Bless Africa). It was an inspiring send-off that meant a lot to them. As Winnie watched Nelson go, 'part of my soul', she says, 'went with him'.

Life without Nelson

Winnie went home to pick up the pieces of her life. She was shattered by the viciousness of the sentence. The first weeks and months she describes as utter hell: 'I fumbled along and tried to adjust. It was extremely difficult'. She was allowed to see Nelson once before he was transferred to Robben Island. In the first six months he was only allowed to write one letter. It was hard enough struggling with the personal loneliness but Winnie also found herself burdened with increasing political responsibility. Every time she said something, it was picked up by the press as an official pronouncement: 'Suddenly I wasn't speaking for myself any more, if I uttered a word it was "MANDELA'S WIFE SAYS", and not only was it Mandela's wife speaking but the "POLICY OF THE AFRICAN NATIONAL CONGRESS SEEMS TO HAVE SHIFTED FROM . . ." – and I hadn't the slightest idea what they were talking about'.

Winnie found this particularly difficult and admits: 'I couldn't handle the situation at first. I couldn't handle myself.' It was difficult to know who to turn to for help. Some of the people whom Winnie had treated as friends turned out to be police informers.

Winnie's banning order made it impossible to continue as a social worker. She tried lots of different jobs but often she would be hired on Monday and fired on Friday. Usually her employer had been warned off by the security police. One manager told her, 'You can keep this job for the rest of your life if you agree to divorce your husband.' It was just as difficult finding a school for the children. As soon as people realised who they were, the children were expelled. People were frightened. Anyone who helped Winnie and her daughters automatically became of interest to the authorities. Friends who took the children to school were picked up for questioning.

Winnie herself was constantly harrassed by the police: 'Our house was an extension of the police station, every day they came. The children were petrified.' From this time on

Nelson Mandela with Walter Sisulu on Robben Island in 1966. As political prisoners they were separated from the others. In the early days conditions were very bad; each isolated in a small cell with inadequate food and clothing. Their first victory was to be allowed out into the yard to break up rocks.

Winnie was in and out of prison and was always worried about her children. In desperation she made the decision to send them away to school. In 1967 Zeni and Zindzi went to boarding school in Swaziland. Zindzi was then seven and Zeni eight. A white friend, Elinor Birley, organised it for Winnie. She, together with some other friends, also paid the fees. The children were used to life without their parents which helped them adjust to boarding school, 'we were so used to being away with friends because Mummy was always in prison.' Sometimes Winnie hardly saw the children during their holidays. Often she was picked up by the police just as they came home from school.

Arrested

One policeman who came to arrest Winnie ended up with a broken neck. He'd come into her bedroom without knocking. 'I had my skirt halfway up and he walked in just like that, he didn't retreat and say excuse me . . . he put his hand on my shoulder. I don't know how he landed on his neck! All I remember is grabbing him and throwing him on the floor.'

The policeman recovered. Winnie was charged with resisting arrest but much to her amazement the court found her not guilty. Her luck did not last. On 12 May 1969, Winnie's door was kicked open in the middle of the night. The children, home from school, were asleep. Security police searched the house, even lifting the children out of bed to search under the bedclothes. Then they announced that Winnie was to be detained. Zeni and Zindzi were driven to their aunt's house and left there. They did not see their mother again for eighteen months.

Chapter 8

'Those Were Horrible Days'

Winnie can hardly bear to recall her eighteen months in prison. It was the treatment she and the other prisoners received that finally forced her to return hatred with hatred.

She was kept in the death cell in Pretoria Central Prison. Twenty-one people had been rounded up at the same time but for months Winnie was unaware of this. She had no idea that there were other detainees in her block. All she could hear from her cell was distant coughing and the faint noise of doors being locked and unlocked: 'Those first few days are the worst in anyone's life, that uncertainty, that insecurity: there is such a sense of hopelessness, the feeling that this is now the end'.

Winnie was to spend 491 days in detention, most of it in solitary confinement. Her cell was small and contained a sanitary bucket, a plastic water bottle and a mug. Sometimes the wardens brought in a little plastic bucket containing water to wash in. This smelt just like the sanitary buckets. There was nothing to wash with, so she had to use her underpants. For a bed there was a mat and three filthy smelly blankets. She found it impossible to make herself comfortable on the cement floor. 'What kept me going in the cells,' she says, 'were the Canadian Air Force exercises for women – I'm addicted to those, I couldn't live without them'.

One day Winnie spent the entire time playing with two ants. She was grateful for their company. She also passed the time by

Talk

They had me on the floor.
The stick came down, down.
They had me crawling and
*   licking their boots.*
'You can talk now,
*   or you can talk later.*
But you'll talk.
Ja, you'll talk and you'll talk
*   and you'll talk.'*

In the morning, the sun came
*   up*
(Or the sun came up and
it was morning).
They bought me a bowl of
*   pap,*
coffee,
cigarettes.
They said – you'll be a good
*   boy.*

Allan Kolski Horwitz

45

undoing one of her blankets and making little ropes from the threads. She would spend days twining them together, and then would undo her work and start all over again. The light was kept on at night, and Winnie, who had suffered from insomnia for some years, found it impossible to sleep. Every day two women guards inspected her cell. She had to stand naked while they examined her body and her clothing.

Winnie spent five days and nights under constant interrogation. On the fifth day she began to have fainting spells. Her body was swollen and she found blood in her urine. Her interrogators threatened her saying, 'you are going to be broken completely, you are shattered, you are a finished woman'. They tried to force Winnie to tell them about people who worked for the ANC. At one point Swanpoel, her interrogator, said to her, 'We have succeeded in telling people that you want to work for us, it hardly makes a difference whether you do or don't.'

Winnie was held for nearly seven months without any contact with the outside world. Nelson's lawyers were frantically trying to find out what had happened to her. Every enquiry was met with silence. Eventually they got an order through the Supreme Court directing that the detainees be given basic facilities. For the first time in two hundred days Winnie was able to wash properly.

In February 1970, ten months after the arrests, the case eventually came to court. Winnie and her co-defendants were found not guilty of the charges of 'illegal political activity', only to be re-arrested before they had even left the court. Finally, in September, they again came to court and again were found not guilty. Although the judge had

That same afternoon the cells were opened, first mine and then four others and we were taken out. I'll never forget the feeling of that moment, a kind of muted consternation when we five women saw each other. There was Winnie Mandela, Rita Ndzanga, Martha Dhlamini, Thokozile Mngoma—and of course we half expected, as our interrogators had said, that the others had agreed to give evidence. But they hadn't. I remember that we hugged each other hard: it was too good to be true. We felt that this was a moment of victory and we were together.

Joyce Sikakane,
A Window On Soweto

Within the first few weeks of her 'freedom' Winnie addressed a meeting of over a thousand people in Durban, where she received a tremendous welcome. She was not deterred by the thought of being rebanned because for Winnie, as long as the situation in South Africa remains unchanged, 'there is really no freedom as such'.

pronounced them free, Winnie's automatic reaction was to turn to go back to her cell. She couldn't believe that this time she could really go home. Her lawyer took her arm and led her out to the waiting crowds.

'Normal life' resumed

While Winnie was in prison Nelson's son by his first marriage had been killed in a car accident. Winnie knew how upset Nelson would be. She was desperate to see him but was refused permission to visit. Two weeks after her release from prison Winnie was placed under a banning order and put under house arrest. Yet again, she had to be at home from 6 p.m. to 6 a.m. and all day at weekends with no visitors.

The government's treatment of Winnie had received some publicity and the refusal to let her visit Nelson had been severely criticised as inhumane. Winnie's next application for a visit, a month later, was granted. Winnie flew the hundreds of miles to Cape Town and took the ferry out to Robben Island. It was two years since she had last seen her husband. Their reunion, through the usual thick glass barrier, lasted only thirty minutes. Back home in Soweto Winnie collapsed; aged only thirty-four, she had a heart attack.

Winnie recovered and her life resumed the old pattern. The police were in and out of the house. They kept up a constant stream of petty charges. Despite watchmen and guard dogs there were frightening attacks on the house. One night Winnie was sleeping with her ten-year-old niece when a noise woke her. She turned the light on. There were three men in the bedroom, one of them coming towards her with a noose in his hand. Winnie leapt out of bed, determined to put up a fight. Fortunately the screams of her niece woke the neighbours and the men fled.

A kind of freedom

In October 1974 Winnie went to prison again. When she came out six months later her banning order expired. After thirteen years she had a kind of freedom. On her first 'unbanned' morning Helen Joseph phoned Winnie. It was their first conversation for five years. 'I said "What will you do, will you come for supper?" She said "Where else would I spend my first night of freedom?" So she came and really that was lovely.'

For ten months Winnie led a relatively normal life. She began to address public meetings again, finding it difficult at first after so many years of enforced silence. She also became involved in community affairs in Soweto. Worried parents, particularly, came to Winnie for help and advice. Throughout this period she had, at last, a fairly well paid job, more in keeping with her professional qualifications than anything she had done for years. She was also continuing to study. Sometimes she spent the weekend working in Helen's house, which was a lot more peaceful than her own. On 16 June 1976 that fragile peace was shattered. A Soweto mother phoned Winnie at work and screamed down the phone, 'Please come, the police are shooting our children.'

I got more liberated in prison. The physical identification with your beliefs is far more satisfying than articulating them on a platform. . . . The whole country is a prison for the black man – and when you are inside, you know why you are there, and the people who put you there also know.

Winnie Mandela,
Part of My Soul

Chapter 9

Soweto

There had been considerable unrest and anxiety in Soweto's schools in the days leading up to 16 June. Many of the school students were influenced by the Black Consciousness Movement which had emerged in the late sixties. As Winnie says, 'when you are deprived, you tend to look down on yourself, too'. The Black Consciousness Movement stopped that. It helped black people regain their pride. 'Black,' Steve Biko and his fellow students insisted, 'is beautiful.'

Steve Biko was the leading spirit in the Black Consciousness Movement. He was determined to make 'blackness, the reason for our oppression, the symbol of our liberation'. On 12 September 1977, he died in police custody as a result of brain damage caused by blows to the head.

The students' anger became focused on a government order that classes in black secondary schools should be taught in Afrikaans. Afrikaans was not only the language of a hated government, it was a language that no one else in the world spoke.

It would only hold back black pupils who wanted to continue their studies outside South Africa.

The Soweto Students Representative Council organised the protest. Twenty thousand children, some still at primary school, marched with their banners. Police vehicles rushed to the scene and tried to stop the demonstration. As a result, a thirteen-year-old schoolboy called Hector Petersen died. He was shot from behind. The streets erupted, the police and army moved in with greater force and the deaths multiplied. Over six hundred people were killed, most of them school students. Winnie says that they were powerless to stop the children.

After 16 June many young people fled the country for military training with the ANC in exile. Another generation had joined the battle.

School students in Soweto begin their march against the use of Afrikaans in their classrooms. Each school marched separately before joining the main body of the demonstration. They all expected the protest to be a peaceful one.

50

Back in Soweto Winnie had joined other community leaders in establishing the Black Parents Association. They acted, when asked, as a mouthpiece for the student leaders who were all on the run. Their main function, however, was to provide medical, legal and financial help as riots, strikes and school boycotts spread all over the country. The authorities appeared to hold Winnie personally responsible for the unrest, maintaining that she was manipulating and directing the struggle of the children. When Winnie was accused of this to her face by a South African officer, she lost her temper. 'She threw a book at him, her shoe, anything and everything she could lay her hands on – "You bloody murderer, killer of our children, and you tell us we started the riots".'

In August 1976 Winnie was imprisoned again. No charges were made and she was released in January 1977, but was immediately placed under house arrest. She went back to her job and in the hours between 6 p.m. and 6 a.m., when she was forbidden to go out, she got on with her studies. In May Winnie was again picked up. This time the punishment was not prison but banishment. She was to be sent to Brandfort, a small Afrikaans town in the Orange Free State where the black people did not even speak the same language as her.

Exile

Winnie and Zindzi, heavily guarded, were escorted to Brandfort police station and then taken to their new 'home'. It made their simple house in Soweto seem like a palace. In Brandfort there was no electricity or sewerage. Their three cell-like rooms had bare earth floors and were filled with rubbish. The

Hector Peterson, the first child to be killed. He was only 13.

The children picked up stones, they used dustbin lids as shields and marched towards machine guns . . . You could smell the gunfire everywhere. Children were dying in the streets, and as they were dying the others marched forward facing guns.

Winnie Mandela,
Part of My Soul

furniture that the authorities had brought from Soweto would not fit in through the door. Cold and tired, on the first night they had no water, no food and no blankets. For Zindzi particularly it was a painful experience, as Winnie describes: 'Worse things have happened to people in the struggle but for a sixteen-year-old girl it was very hard to take. It was the hardest thing for me to take as a mother – that your commitment affects those who are very dear to you.'

Brandfort is a small, conservative town. The black people there live in great poverty, and, as Zindzi commented, 'I thought Soweto was deprived until I went to Brandfort'. The blacks had been warned to keep away from Winnie and Zindzi, on threat of arrest. They did not dare approach the Mandelas during the day but before long food parcels were being left outside the house at night.

Winnie's presence electrified the

neighbourhood. The whites had never come across a black person like her. Winnie used shops that no black person would go into. She used the 'whites only' entrances to the police station and the post office. Others began to follow her example:

'When I went to the supermarket there were these huge Afrikaans-speaking women. When they saw me they used to run out and stay out until I finished my shopping. The "Bantus" didn't get into the supermarket, they had these little windows through which they were supposed to buy. But once I started shopping there the blacks went in too, and then I would deliberately take an hour to get whatever I needed – even if it was only a bar of soap – and I enjoyed seeing these women waiting outside.'

Winnie caused such upheaval that at one point the whites asked the Minister of Justice to have her removed. She was having a 'bad effect' on the local blacks.

The black people would not have agreed. Winnie is, as her daughter says, 'a born social worker' and she threw herself into improving their living conditions. She was shocked by what she had found: 'In my childhood in the Transkei I lived among poverty; in my social work in Johannesburg I saw even worse poverty, but never in my life had I imagined conditions as grim as those in this Brandfort ghetto.'

There was very little work for the blacks in Brandfort. Many people could not afford to eat properly. Winnie noticed that funerals of babies and young children were particularly common. Children walked miles to school

People often seem to have given up the struggle . . . Now this sense of defeat is basically what we are fighting against. People must not give in to the hardship of life. People must develop a hope. People must develop some form of security to be together to look at their problems, and people must in this way build up their humanity. This is the point of Black Consciousness.

Steve Biko

and back on an empty stomach. For some families, the main – sometimes only – meal of the day was mealie-pap, a sort of porridge, and salted water. Winnie organised a crèche and a soup kitchen and started a garden project encouraging people to grow their own vegetables. Her home became a clinic and an unofficial welfare centre.

One white family in the area became her friends. Piet de Waal, the only lawyer in Brandfort, agreed to act for Winnie. His wife Adele befriended her. She lent Winnie books, offered her the use of their bathroom and cooked hot meals for Winnie and Zindzi. As a result of her kindness and affection for Winnie, Adele was ignored by the rest of the white community. Winnie was the first black

Winnie and Zindzi awaiting banishment to Brandfort in 1977.

person the de Waals had got to know socially. It was quite a shock to them to find that the famous Winnie Mandela was not the ogre the authorities had warned them against.

Back to Soweto

In October 1982 Piet de Waal called at Winnie's house on business. He found her in bed with a raging fever. She was seriously ill with an infected leg that had been allowed to fester. Permission would have to be asked before she could be admitted to an all-white hospital in the nearest large town of Bloemfontein. Winnie refused to go and insisted that she be flown to a multi-racial clinic in Johannesburg. But she needed a permit to leave Brandfort. Her lawyer and doctor warned that the delay might cost her her life. Winnie was prepared to wait. The authorities gave in. They did not want to be blamed for her death. The doctor was already saying that Winnie's primitive living conditions had caused the rapid spread of the infection.

So, after five years in exile, Winnie was flown back to Johannesburg. She spent seven weeks in hospital. Although she was incapable of moving, the security police watched her constantly. When she left hospital, defying her banning order, she went to convalesce in her own home in Soweto. She felt too weak to cope on her own in Brandfort. People came to see her in their hundreds.

Winnie was struck by the increased bitterness in Soweto. Since 1976 resentment had hardened. People were more determined than ever to gain their rights, and more likely to fight for them.

The people have risen, the people are in revolt. The people have had enough of this apartheid poison, of the apartheid lie that 'alles sal regkom (all will come right)'. The people won't take another sjambokking – they are hitting back, they are shooting back. They are hurling hand grenades, they are making their own Molotov cocktails. They are getting adept at it from as early as eight years of age. Yes, a guerilla has no age. He has been getting younger since the 1976 Students' Revolt.

Mothobi Mutloatse,
'A Letter from Soweto'

Chapter 10

The Eighties

In May 1984 Winnie went to visit Nelson with Zeni and Zeni's youngest child. When they arrived at the prison Winnie was summoned into the office. Her first thought was that Nelson was ill. But the news was good – from now on she would be allowed 'contact' visits. For the first time in twenty two years she could touch her husband. 'They hoped that we would adjust well to the new kind of prison visit,' Winnie recalls. 'They knew that seeing someone, a loved one, after so many years, at close range might be traumatic. They hoped it wouldn't be so. This is what they had decided . . . It was about time, too. There was really nothing to be grateful for.' For Winnie it was an experience that is impossible to put into words, 'fantastic and hurting at the same time'. Throughout the visit Nelson clung to his grandson.

Winnie and her two daughters after a visit to Nelson. It was the first time they had been together as a family for twenty-three years. Zeni and Zindzi were not allowed to visit their father until they were sixteen.

Winnie was still living in Brandfort. Over the years her household had increased. Zeni's three children and Zindzi's two were frequent visitors. In the summer of 1985 Winnie's life was threatened yet again. The house in Brandfort was petrol-bombed. No one was ever caught. The Mandelas and their friends are certain that the security police must have been involved. Winnie left Brandfort and returned to Soweto, refusing to be moved.

Counting the cost

The years of struggle and of separation from her husband have taken their toll on Winnie. Her daughter Zeni says that her mother has always had a strong character: 'The more you push her the more she pushes back. But she has definitely hardened because of what she has been through.' Winnie's experience in solitary confinement changed her finally from a social worker whose instinct was to preserve life to a woman who could say, 'In defence of my principles I know I would fire.' She has come to believe that the time for peaceful change in South Africa is running out.

In her house in Soweto, the house that Nelson took her to as a young bride all those years ago, Winnie is always surrounded by people. The phone never stops ringing. Children, five of them her grandchildren, tumble in and out. Although her banning order has been lifted and she is now 'as free as any other black South African', she is constantly watched. Black and white alike keep their eyes on her. Recently the white community in particular was horrified when she was quoted apparently encouraging violence, – 'With our necklaces and our matches we will liberate South Africa'.

After spending a day in Brandfort with her, one detects that her vivacious extroversion and irrepressible humour is but a mask behind which is hidden a deep heartache, a bitterness, a smouldering anger about the tragedies of her own life, her 22 year separation from her husband and about the daily experiences of her black compatriots in apartheid society.

From a newspaper article by J. H. P. Serfontein

Necklacing refers to the practice of placing a burning tyre around someone's neck, which is a revenge sometimes taken on black informers. Winnie was not suggesting that actions like this are admirable. But she and many others can understand, and feel, the anger that unleashes such violence.

Over the years, partly as a consequence of her banishment to Brandfort, Winnie has become increasingly separated from her old friends. This makes her even more vulnerable to criticism and speculation. There was controversy over her decision to build a house in the so-called 'Beverley Hills' area of Soweto. Winnie saw it as a tribute to Nelson but in a country where many black people live in great poverty the new building attracted a lot of resentment. The authorities, with their network of spies and informers, are not slow to exploit any disputes among the black community.

Helen Joseph, now in her eighties, expresses the concern about Winnie felt by many of her old friends when she says, 'There's a lot of criticism now that's coming out. I'm sure that if people really understood the circumstances they would feel differently about it. We're living in a time of extreme tension and people's patience is not inexhaustive. They draw conclusions and vent them on people.'

Black South Africans live their lives under constant pressure and feelings can run high. The white government has become skilled at manipulating them.

The Mandela myth
In many ways Winnie is isolated – despite the people surrounding her. She has become as much a myth as a real person. She is

I asked a couple I had not met before what it was like to live in Soweto now . . . 'In your street one day it's all right. The next day . . . you'll die. It's like Beirut.' . . .
It's more like Beirut than he knew. I remember a film I once saw where the camera moved from destruction and its hateful cacophony in the streets to a villa where people were lunching on a terrace, and there were birds and flowers. That's what it's like.

Nadine Gordimer, A Letter From Johannesburg

Mandela's wife, the 'Mother of the Nation', the focus of never-ending press attention. Her physical beauty and ability to express herself powerfully pushed her increasingly into the limelight. As an attractive woman she has of course been seized on by the press and probably also promoted by her own comrades.

Many other women in South Africa have had to suffer very much in the way that Winnie has. They also have been imprisoned, persecuted, separated from husband and children. Many have had worse material conditions, and have seen those they loved

Winnie with two of her grandchildren at a press conference in her Soweto home. The date is 18 July 1986, her husband's birthday, and part of their 28-year-old wedding cake still awaits his release and the completion of their marriage ceremony.

59

killed or exiled. They have also shown great courage and determination. Yet they have gone largely unnoticed in the outside world. But perhaps Winnie's fame, despite the advantages it brings of financial help from well-wishers, and status, has in many ways made her life even more difficult. For years she and Nelson have been the focal point of the struggle for black independence. For Winnie it must have been lonely. A weaker woman would have found the strain of just living up to the legend unbearable.

The present day

Winnie is now studying political science and industrial sociology at Witwatersrand University in Johannesburg. She sits in the class, a grandmother, and borrows Zindzi's essays. She is keen to achieve a high standard of education in order to be useful in a new South Africa. She also feels the need for a new order in her own life; 'Because of the pressures the country imposes on people like myself it became impossible to tie myself down to one particular thing at a time. The demands were so much that I hardly had a minute for the family and for myself . . . I feared exhausting myself and drying myself up.'

Nearly thirty years after her marriage to 'the struggle, not the man', Winnie fights on. It is being part of that struggle which keeps her going.

'I get my inspiration from the very knowledge that one is not alone. The knowledge that the struggle is an international struggle for the dignity of man and that you are part of the family of man – this alone sustains you.'

She is convinced that the cause she, Nelson and thousands of others have dedicated their lives to will eventually triumph but she is concerned that her generation have nothing to offer the next one; 'We cannot give them any vision of tomorrow and say for definite this is what we can offer you. We remain as oppressed as we were ten years ago, we remain as oppressed as we were twenty-six years ago when the people's leaders were sent to jail.' And yet the achievements of her generation cannot be dismissed in this way. It may still take a long time but it is they who have laid the foundation of freedom in South Africa. They have paid in one way or another with their lives and have demonstrated to the world that the cause of black South Africa is also the cause of justice and harmony.

White South Africa . . . will eventually have to learn – whether they like it or not – that this country will be non-racial and that this country belongs to all who live in it.
Amandla Ngawetu.
Power to the People.

Winnie Mandela

Johannesburg, 1986.

TIME CHART

Events in Winnie Mandela's life

1934 26th September, Winnie Madikizela born, in the Transkei.
1953 Winnie arrives in Johannesburg to train as a social worker.
1955 She starts work at Baragwanath Hospital in Soweto.
1956 Winnie is introduced to Nelson Mandela.
1958 Winnie and Nelson marry. Winnie takes part in a women's anti-pass demonstration and is arrested.
1959 The Mandelas' first daughter, Zenani, born.
1960 Mandelas' second daughter, Zindziswa, born.
1961 Nelson decides to work 'underground'.
1962 Nelson arrested and sentenced to five years imprisonment.
1963 Winnie receives her first banning order.
1964 Nelson sentenced to life imprisonment.
1965 The government serves a five-year banning order on Winnie. As a result she loses her job.
1967 Winnie charged with resisting arrest. Found not guilty but then jailed for violating her banning order.
1969 Winnie is arrested and spends 491 days in jail. She is charged with furthering the activities of the ANC.
1970 14 September, Winnie finally acquitted.
30 September, she is served with another five-year banning order and in October has a heart attack.
1974 Winnie jailed for violating her banning order.
1975 Winnie's banning order suspended.
1976 Winnie imprisoned after Soweto massacre.
1977 Winnie's banning order renewed and she is banished to Brandfort.
Zenani Mandela marries Prince Thumbumuzi of Swaziland.
1981 Winnie's banning order renewed for another five years.
1982 Winnie ill and returns to hospital in Johannesburg.
1984 Winnie has first 'contact' visit to Nelson.
1985 A gasolene bomb destroys Winnie's house in Brandfort and she returns to Soweto.
1986 Winnie's banning order expires. She had been banned almost continuously for over 24 years.

Events in South African History (1910–1987)

1910 Britain grants independance to South Africa and the new Union of South Africa is formed.

1912 The South African Native National Congress founded.

1913 The Native Lands Act secures most of the land for whites, reserving only 7% for African tribal ownership. Black people cannot own land as individuals.

1923 South African Native National Congress changes its name to the African National Congress (ANC) and adopts a national anthem and flag.

1944 ANC youth league formed. Founder members include Nelson Mandela, Oliver Tambo and Walter Sisulu.

1948 White electorate vote the National Party into power on a policy of apartheid.

1950 Population Registration Act and Group Areas Act classify everyone as Black, White, Asian or Coloured and restrict their living areas accordingly.

1952 The Defiance Campaign.

1953 Bantu Education Act.

1955 Freedom Charter adopted at Congress of the People.

1960 Massacre at Sharpeville.

1961 Military wing of ANC formed.

1962 Nelson Mandela arrested and sentenced to five years in prison.

1964 Rivonia Trial. Nelson and several other ANC leaders sentenced to life imprisonment.

1976 Massacre at Soweto.

1977 Steve Biko dies while in police custody.

1984 New constitution in South Africa opens up some political representation to Indian and Coloured South Africans. A successful boycott campaign means that only one in five Coloured voters and one in seven Indians actually vote.

1984–1986 Increased awareness of apartheid abroad. Issue of sanctions becomes increasingly prominent.

1985 Mixed Marriages Act repealed but Group Areas Act remains in force. Couples can marry but not live together.

1987 In the white elections voters re-elect the National Party, the more liberal Progressive Federal Party loses support.

1988 February, in the most repressive action for 10 years the government serves banning orders on many black protest groups and their leaders.

Index

BIBLIOGRAPHY

Sources
Part of My Soul Winnie Mandela (Penguin, 1985)
Call Me Woman Ellen Kuzwayo (Women's Press, 1985)
Sometimes When it Rains (Pandora Press, 1987)
A Window on Soweto Joyce Sikhane (IDAF, 1977)
Move Your Shadow Joseph Lelyveld (Michael Joseph, 1986)
Biko Donald Woods (Paddington Press, 1977)

Further Reading
Cry, the Beloved Country Alan Paton (Penguin, 1958)
Journey to Jo'burg Beverley Naidoo (British Defence and Aid Fund for Southern Africa, 1985)
Chaka Thomas Mofolo (Heinemann Educational, 1981)
The Children of Soweto Mbulelo Vizikhungo Mzamane (Longman, 1982)
Mother of a Nation Nancy Harrison (Grafton, 1986)
Nelson Mandela Mary Benson (Penguin, 1986)
South Africa: A Different Kind of War Julie Frederikse (James Curry, 1986)
A History of South Africa Learner Pack (Development Education Centre, 1986)
Apartheid: A Graphic Guide Donald Woods and Mike Bostock (Camden Press, 1986)
The Child is not Dead a teaching resource (ILEA and BDAF)

Videos
Winnie Mandela (distributed by The Other Cinema)
You have Struck a Rock (distributed by The Other Cinema)

Resource Centres
International Defence and Aid Fund for Southern Africa (IDAF), Canon Collins House, 64 Essex Road, London N1 8LR.
Anti-Apartheid Movement, 13 Mandela Street, London N1 0DW.

The publishers wish to thank the following agencies and photographers for supplying photographs for this book:

Afrapix pages 2, 56 (P. auf der Heyde), 59 (Anna Zieminski), 61 (Gill de Vlieg); Bailey's African Photo Archives page 30 (Bob Gosani), Camera Press pages 9 above and below (James Barr), 21 (John Seymour), 31 (Eli Weinberg), 49 left (Michael Ryan); John Hillelson pages 6 (Ian Berry), 17 (Ernest Cole); I.D.A.F. cover above (Caroline Schuten) and below, pages 2, 12, 13, 19, 24, 25 (Eli Weinberg), 27 (Eli Weinberg), 28 (Eli Weinberg), 29, 32, 35, 36, 41, 43, 47, 49 (right), 50, 52, 54; Popperfoto page 16.